Usborne
Build your own
DRAGONS
Sticker Book

Designed by Marc Maynard
Written by Simon Tudhope
Illustrated by Gong Studios

Contents

Ravenhold is a land filled with dragons and magic. Many of the most dangerous and powerful dragons are illustrated in this book. Some have human riders, and some can never be tamed. Once you've read about a dragon, you can look at the map below to see where it lives.

Drakash

High above Ravenhold, Drakash burns like a second sun. He makes his own lightning and lets it flow through his veins. Then... CRACK! His target disappears in a flash of light.

STATISTICS

- **Attack power:** 8
- **Speed:** 7
- **Size:** 7
- **Age:** 130 years old
- **Realm:** The Urghar Wildlands

Murgarna

The witch-queen of Morven Castle has turned herself into a dragon. Perched high on the clifftops, an unearthly sound rips from her throat. It reaches into the minds of the soldiers below, and drives them wild with fear. As the army scatters, she tips back her head and unleashes a victorious cry.

STATISTICS

- **Attack power:** 9
- **Speed:** 5
- **Size:** 6
- **Age:** 220 years old
- **Realm:** Morven Island

Parsek

Stonewall is under siege, and Parsek is the people's best hope. Faster than a speeding arrow he carries a messenger over the enemy soldiers. Together, they'll fly to the four corners of the kingdom and raise an army to save the city.

STATISTICS

- **Attack power:** 5
- **Speed:** 10
- **Size:** 6
- **Age:** 50 years old
- **Realm:** Stonewall

Endelung

The ocean churns as a monstrous creature bursts from the deep. It looms over the ship below, and a lightning flash reveals its face. The captain cries: "It's Endelung – pirate's doom! She'll drown us all to steal our loot!"

Rangar

Meet the fiercest and most powerful dragon in the kingdom of Ravenhold. He drinks lava from volcanoes and burns down whole forests with a single blast.

STATISTICS

- **Attack power:** 10
- **Speed:** 6
- **Size:** 9
- **Age:** 280 years old
- **Realm:** The Lost Caverns

Wugmeer

In the steaming heart of Gloamlands Swamp, Wugmeer lies completely still. He looks just like a rotting log. But his eyes are following something long and red, moving underwater. With a whip of his tail he brings a snake to the surface... straight to his waiting jaws!

STATISTICS

- **Attack power:** 4
- **Speed:** 7
- **Size:** 5
- **Age:** 300 years old
- **Realm:** Gloamlands Swamp

Magaloki

Most people in Ravenhold think this three-headed dragon is a myth – but they're wrong. Magaloki really does exist, and really does have three heads. The first breathes ice, the second breathes fire, and the third head turns you to stone.

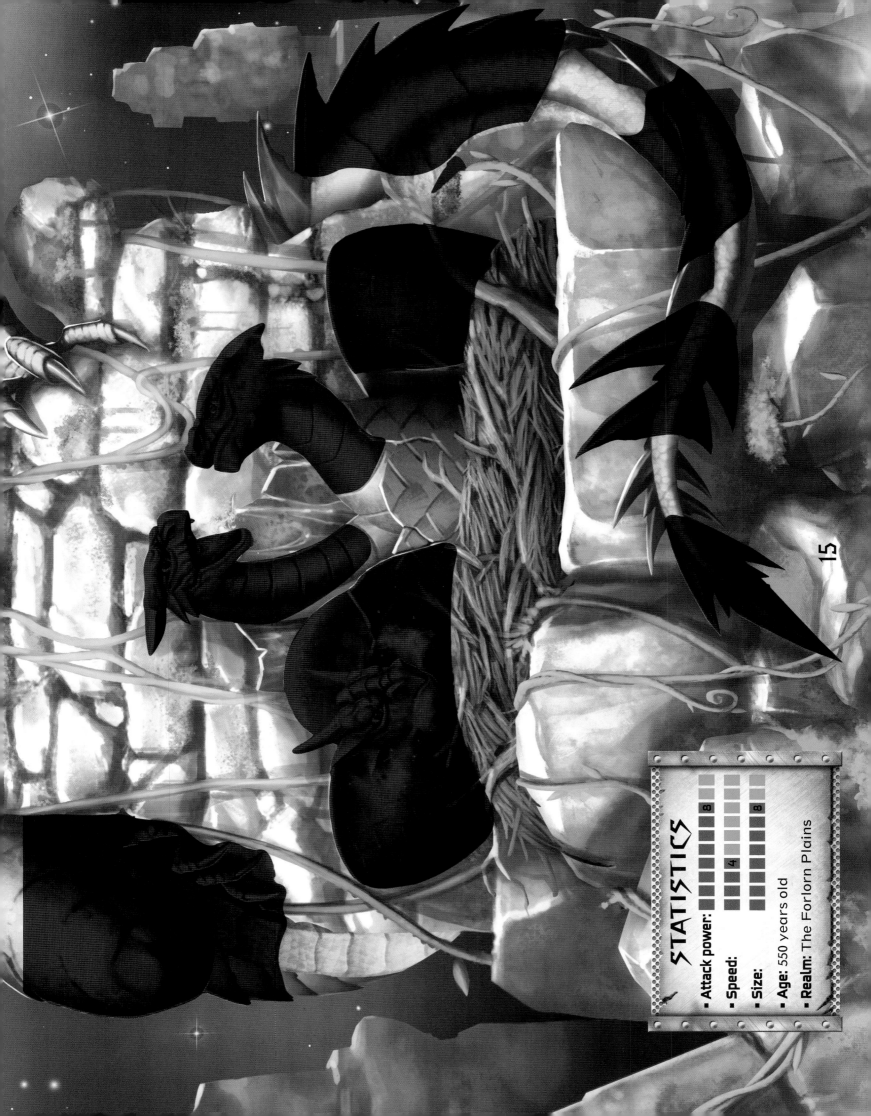

STATISTICS

- **Attack power:** 8
- **Speed:** 4
- **Size:** 8
- **Age:** 550 years old
- **Realm:** The Forlorn Plains

The Drakavi

As night approaches the Drakavi awaken.
Down below, an explorer sees hundreds of
little lights appear in the treetops. But then
the lights start to swirl and grow... and blink.
Those aren't lights – they're eyes! As the
swarm descends, he starts to run.

- **Attack power:** 6
- **Speed:** 8
- **Size:** 2
- **Age:** life-expectancy of 30 years
- **Realm:** Grimwold Forest

Bagudush

The walls of Pellanor have stood for hundreds of years, but they've never faced anything like Bagudush. With a fearsome roar and a swing of her tail, she sends an ancient watchtower crashing to earth.

STATISTICS

- **Attack power:** 8
- **Speed:** 6
- **Size:** 7
- **Age:** 180 years old
- **Realm:** The Luru Plains

Stalagar

At first, the cavern looks empty...
except for the treasure. But touch
a single coin or gem, and the icicles
start to creak and crack. Stalagar
rears up from the floor! He comes
to life to protect his hoard, and can
freeze you solid with a single breath.

STATISTICS

- **Attack power:** 7
- **Speed:** 2
- **Size:** 8
- **Age:** 460 years old
- **Realm:** The Frozen Sea

Slygarr

Deep underground, a sorcerer found this dragon's bones and brought it back to life. A green fire kindled in the empty skull, and a soft voice hissed: "I am Slygarr, queen of all dragons – and now I shall rule again!"

STATISTICS

- **Attack power:** 9
- **Speed:** 7
- **Size:** 7
- **Age:** 960 years old
- **Realm:** The Dark Mountains

Glossary

- **kindled:** started burning
- **lava:** incredibly hot, liquid rock that erupts from a volcano. When it cools, it turns back into rock.
- **loot:** stolen treasure
- **myth:** something that doesn't exist or didn't happen
- **rears up:** rises

- **siege:** when soldiers surround a castle so that no one can get in or out, and the people inside starve
- **sorcerer:** a wizard
- **tamed:** trained to live with humans

Edited by Sam Taplin

Digital manipulation by Keith Furnival

First published in 2019 by Usborne Publishing Limited, 83-85 Saffron Hill, London EC1N 8RT, United Kingdom. usborne.com Copyright © 2019 Usborne Publishing Limited. The name Usborne and the Balloon logo are registered trade marks of Usborne Publishing Limited.

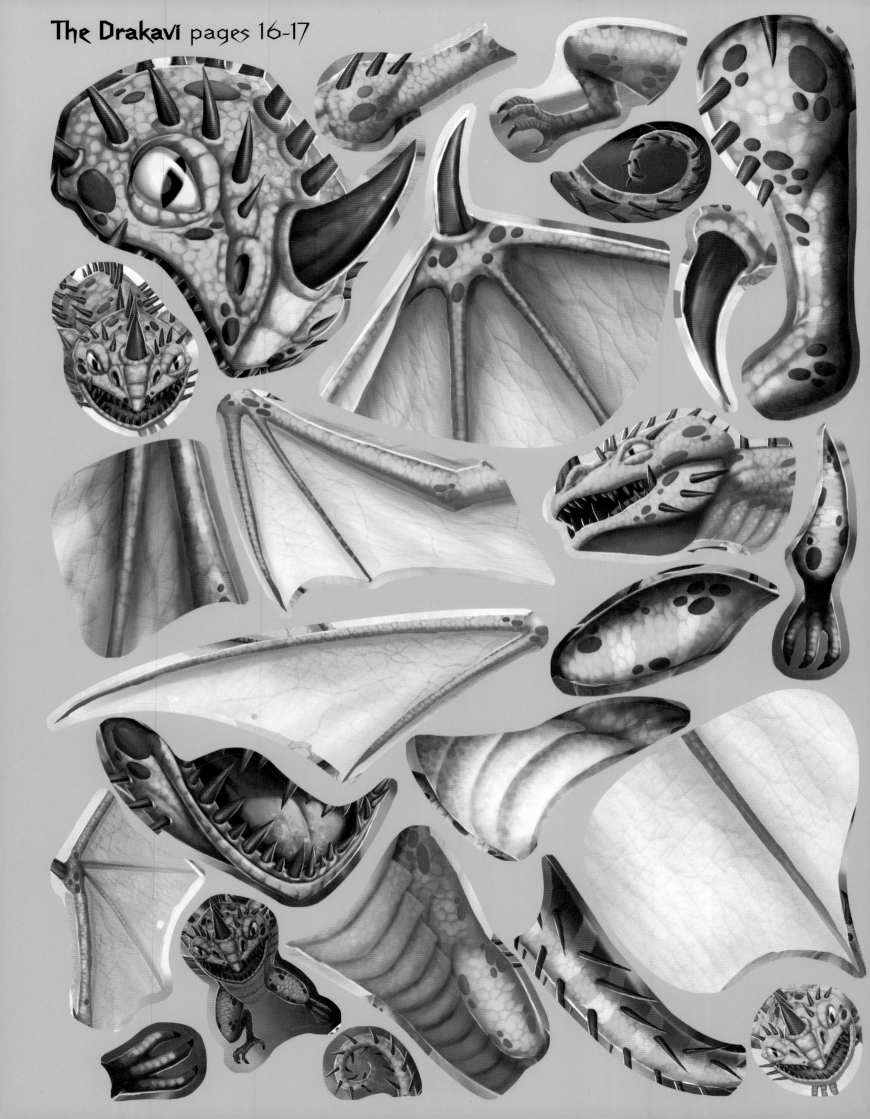

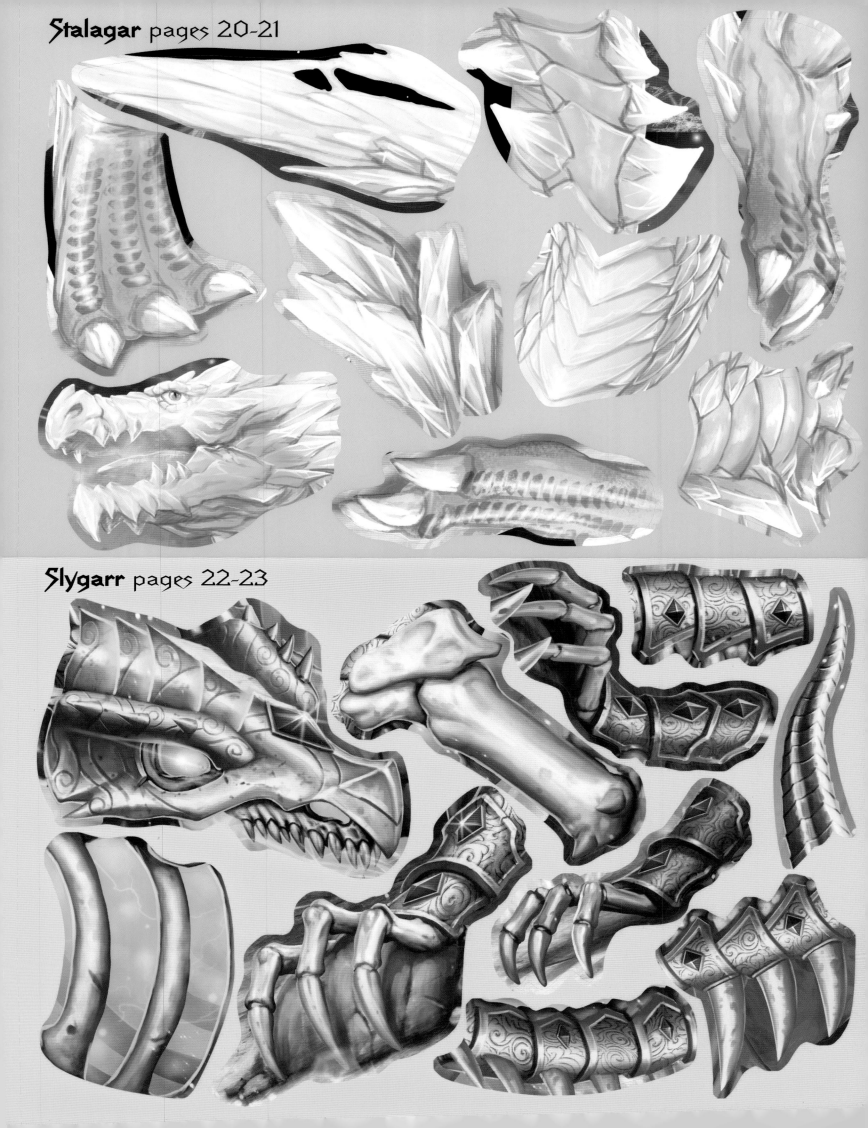

Stalagar pages 20-21

Slygarr pages 22-23